Garfield
Fat Cat
3 Pack

BY: JIM DAVIS

BALLANTINE BOOKS · NEW YORK

ISBN: 0-345-38385-0

Manufactured in the United States of America

First Edition: March 1993

10 9 8 7 6 5 4 3 2 1

Garfield at large

BY: JIM DAVIS

LOOK INSIDE THIS BOOK
AND SEE THIS CAT...
• EAT LASAGNA
• CHASE DOGS
• DESTROY A MAILMAN
• LAUGH; CRY, FFFT
• SHRED HIS OWNER
• AND MUCH, MUCH MORE!

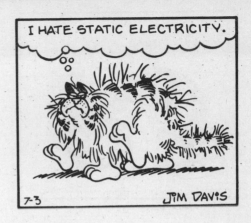

AH, A CURTAIN UPON WHICH TO SHARPEN MY CLAWS.

© 1978 United Feature Syndicate, Inc.

7-7

I HATE DOUBLE-KNIT.

JIM DAVIS

DEAR GARFIELD:
BELIEVE IT OR NOT, I AM AN UGLY KITTEN! OH, I DO ALL THE THINGS "CUTE" KITTENS DO...PLAY WITH YARN AND SUCH, BUT I DON'T GET ANY ATTENTION. WHAT CAN I DO?

MUD FENCE

DEAR "MUD":
YOU'RE TRYING TOO HARD TO BE CUTE. YOU'LL GET MORE ATTENTION IF YOU JUST BE YOURSELF...

7-8

AND SHARPEN YOUR CLAWS ON THE LIVING ROOM DRAPES.

JIM DAVIS   © 1978 United Feature Syndicate, Inc.

7/23

DON'T TRY LOOKING CUTE AT ME, GARFIELD. YOU STILL CAN'T HAVE ANY OF MY STEAK.

© 1978 United Feature Syndicate, Inc.

7-30

JIM DAVIS

LYMAN, YOU GOTTA HOUSEBREAK ODIE

HOW?

© 1978 United Feature Syndicate. Inc.

8-16

SWAT HIM WITH SOMETHING

WITH WHAT?

JIM DAVIS

© 1978 United Feature Syndicate. Inc.

8-17

PAT PAT PAT PAT

JIM DAVIS

8-25

JIM DAVIS

SPLOOCH!

8-26

HELP YOURSELF TO THE LASAGNA, GARFIELD.

JIM DAVIS

JIM DAVIS

© 1978 United Feature Syndicate, Inc.

9-6

JIM DAVIS

HEE-HEE-HEE

9-7

HA-HA-HA-HA-HA

JIM DAVIS

PURRRR

PURRR!

HAVE SOME LASAGNA, GARFIELD...

PURRRR

© 1978 United Feature Syndicate, Inc. 9-13

JIM DAVIS

© 1978 United Feature Syndicate, Inc.

CRINKLE RUSTLE CRINKLE

GARFIELD, GET OUT OF THE TRASH

JIM DAVIS 9-14

JIM DAVIS

© 1978 United Feature Syndicate, Inc.

SLAM!

9-17

VETERINARY CLINIC

SOMEHOW, THEY ALWAYS KNOW.

9-25

FWIP!

FLUFF FLUFF

GARFIELD! TIME TO EAT!

JIM DAVIS

I HATE MONDAYS.

ALL DOGS SHOULD BE BANNED FROM OUR COUNTRY...

JIM DAVIS

THEY ARE NOISY, SILLY, SLOPPY, RUDE...

9-26

AND THEY'RE RUSTING OUR NATION'S FIRE HYDRANTS.

10-2

I HATE MONDAYS

JIM DAVIS

I WONDER IF I SHOULD PICK UP ANYTHING FOR GARFIELD FROM THE PET STORE

HOW ABOUT A SCRATCHING POST?

JIM DAVIS

GOOD IDEA. I'LL GET HIM ONE

10-3

BLESS YOU!

SCRATCH
SCRATCH
SCRATCH
SCRATCH
SCRATCH
SCRATCH
SCRATCH
SCRATCH
SCRATCH
SCRATCH
SCRATCH
SCRATCH
SCRATCH
SCRATCH

BLINK!

I WIN AGAIN

JIM DAVIS   10-15

I COULDN'T FACE LIFE AS A DECLAWED PERSON. SO I'LL JUST STICK MY HEAD IN THIS OVEN AND END IT ALL

10-18

STUPID ELECTRIC STOVE

JIM DAVIS

JON'S GONNA HAVE ME DECLAWED

10-19

WHAT A FRIGHTENING THOUGHT...

GOING THROUGH LIFE UNARMED

JIM DAVIS

GET AWAY FROM MY FOOD, BEAR!

I JUST YELLED AT A TEDDY BEAR

10-25

JIM DAVIS

NO, GARFIELD. I WILL NOT KISS YOUR TEDDY BEAR GOOD NIGHT

10-26

SMACK

JIM DAVIS

FOUR PLY, STEEL-BELTED, RADIAL RETREAD TENNY PUMPS

ZOOOOOM!

11-3

JIM DAVIS

11-4

ZIP!

THAT HURT ME MORE THAN IT DID HIM

JIM DAVIS

© 1978 United Feature Syndicate, Inc.

BUZZ
SAW
SAW
SCRATCH
SCRATCH
CUT
CUT
BZZZ

11-12

JIM DAVIS

© 1978 United Feature Syndicate, Inc.

CATS NEED A BALANCED DIET

MEAT, EGGS, FRUIT, BREAD, VEGETABLES...

AND AN OCCASIONAL BOSTON FERN FOR DESSERT

11-15 JIM DAVIS

11-16

OH NO! JON GOT A ROCKING CHAIR!

© 1978 United Feature Syndicate, Inc. JIM DAVIS

AS LONG AS THERE IS ONE ROCKING CHAIR LEFT IN THIS WORLD, NO CAT'S TAIL IS SAFE

MY ROCKING CHAIR!

YOUR KINDLING

© 1978 United Feature Syndicate, Inc.

© 1978 United Feature Syndicate, Inc.

BRRR!

YAWN!

12-3

I KNOW YOU'RE IN THERE SOMEWHERE, GARFIELD!... OUT!!!

NEXT TIME I'LL LEAVE A WAKE-UP CALL AT THE DESK

JIM DAVIS   © 1978 United Feature Syndicate, Inc.

NOW, BEHAVE YOURSELF IN THE GROCERY STORE, GARFIELD

JIM DAVIS

I THINK I JUST TURNED A BULL LOOSE IN A CHINA SHOP

12-6

© 1978 United Feature Syndicate, Inc.

THAT'S THE LAST TIME I TAKE YOU TO THE GROCERY STORE, GARFIELD

I'VE NEVER BEEN SO HUMILIATED IN ALL MY LIFE

12-7

SO I ATE THE PASTRY SECTION, BIG DEAL.

JIM DAVIS   © 1978 United Feature Syndicate, Inc.

DARN

© 1978 United Feature Syndicate, Inc.

THAT WAS TOO EASY

JiM DAViS

WHEN ODIE COMES BY I'M GOING TO ROUND OFF THAT POINTY HEAD OF HIS

SLURP!

© 1978 United Feature Syndicate, Inc.

HOW CAN YOU WIN AGAINST SOMEONE WHO DOESN'T EVEN KNOW THE RULES OF THE GAME?

JiM DAViS

© 1978 United Feature Syndicate Inc

HERE, ODIE!

12-10

JIM DAVIS

ISN'T IT A LITTLE COLD TO TAKE ODIE FOR A WALK?

NONSENSE!

THINGS TO DO:
1. wash car
2. do laundry

12-11

3. and brush Garfield

© 1978 United Feature Syndicate, Inc.

JIM DAVIS

I OWN A CAT

12-12

© 1978 United Feature Syndicate, Inc.

AND WHEN YOU OWN A CAT, EATING A NORMAL MEAL TAKES ON AN ALL-NEW PERSPECTIVE

KNOWING THAT SOMEWHERE IN THERE IS A CAT HAIR WITH YOUR NAME ON IT

JIM DAVIS

12-18

JiM DAViS

ZZZZZZ

YAWN!

WHAT A HECK OF A WAY TO WAKE UP

© 1978 United Feature Syndicate, Inc.

12-19

© 1978 United Feature Syndicate, Inc.

JiM DAViS

I KNOW CATS ARE FAST, BUT **THAT'S** RIDICULOUS

HO-HO-HO

© 1978 United Feature Syndicate

WHUMP!

LET'S SEE, GIFTS FOR JON, LYMAN AND ODIE

HMMM

OH YES, AND GARFIELD

JIM DAVIS

12-24

HOW COULD I EVER FORGET, GARFIELD...

ONLY KID IN THE WORLD TO ASK FOR 20 POUNDS OF LASAGNA

POW!

JIM DAVIS

WHAT WOULD YOU LIKE FOR BREAKFAST, GARFIELD?

A CUP OF COFFEE, A DANISH AND THE NEWSPAPER

HAVE A WARM BOWL OF MILK

YOU PEOPLE DON'T GIVE US CATS ANY CREDIT!

JIM DAVIS

1-2

LOOK WHAT MY MOTHER MADE FOR YOU, GARFIELD

1-8

THERE, HOW'S THAT?

IT'S NICE AND WARM

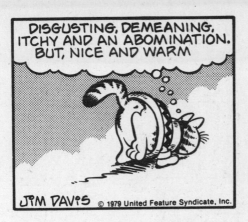

DISGUSTING, DEMEANING, ITCHY AND AN ABOMINATION. BUT, NICE AND WARM

JIM DAVIS © 1979 United Feature Syndicate, Inc.

WOULD YOU JUST LOOK AT THIS? JON'S MAKING ME WEAR A KITTY SWEATER

© 1979 United Feature Syndicate, Inc.

JIM DAVIS

PEOPLE DRESS THEIR PETS UP BECAUSE IT MAKES THEM LOOK LIKE LITTLE PEOPLE. WELL, I'M **NOT** A LITTLE PERSON, I'M A **CAT**

1-9

FOR INSTANCE, I LIKE A PINCH OF CATNIP IN MY MORNING CUP OF COFFEE

HERE HE COMES. SAY SOMETHING NICE

© 1979 United Feature Syndicate, Inc.   1-10

LOOKIN' GOOD, GARFIELD

SHARP SWEATER, OL' BUDDY

SAD

LOOKS LIKE A MEATBALL IN TRACTION

JIM DAVIS

I WAS FEELING PRETTY PUNK ABOUT HAVING TO WEAR THIS SWEATER....

© 1979 United Feature Syndicate, Inc.

UNTIL I SAW ODIE'S NEW OUTFIT

1-11

JIM DAVIS

1-12

1-13

1-15

GARFIELD, YOU SHOULDN'T CHASE THE MAILMAN LIKE THAT

NOW WHAT WOULD YOU DO WITH HIM IF YOU ACTUALLY CAUGHT HIM?

I'D EAT HIM

GARFIELD, YOU KNOW CATS CAN'T DRINK...

1-16

...COFFEE

SLURP!

FILL'ER UP

WELL, I'LL BE DIPPED

JIM DAVIS

JIM DAVIS

IT'S AMAZING HOW WE'VE GROWN TO UNDERSTAND ONE ANOTHER

1-17

LOOK, GARFIELD, A MOUSE!

1-18

EEEK!

JIM DAVIS

Garfield gains weight

BY: JIM DAVIS

"This is the funniest book I've ever read...."

—JIM DAVIS

"This is the funniest book he's ever read...."

—CAROLYN DAVIS, Jim's Wife

"Spectacular...blockbuster ...a sure bestseller."

—JULIE HAMILTON, Jim's Business Manager

"...really average."

—VALETTE HILDEBRAND, Jim's Assistant

"It's such a nice book. He's such a nice boy."

—BETTY DAVIS, Jim's Mother

"This is the best book I ever read. This is the only book I ever read."

—DAVE "DOC" DAVIS, Jim's Brother

"This should do 'til he finds work."

—JAMES W. DAVIS, Jim's Father

"...goo, goo...ha, ha, ha."

—ALEX DAVIS, Jim's Son

© 1981 United Feature Syndicate, Inc.

TELEVISION CAN BE HABIT FORMING

© 1979 United Feature Syndicate, Inc.

JIM DAVIS

I'VE BEEN WATCHING IT ALL DAY

1-23

WOULD YOU LIKE ME TO TURN THE TV ON, GARFIELD?

THAT WOULD BE NICE

© 1979 United Feature Syndicate, Inc.

© 1979 United Feature Syndicate, Inc.

JIM DAVIS

1-28

© 1979 United Feature Syndicate, Inc.

2-4

LET'S SEE... IODINE, BAND-AIDS, GAUZE, BULLWHIP, SMALL STRAIT-JACKET, HELMET, PAN, SHAMPOO, GLOVES, RINSE, CONDITIONER, BLOW DRYER, BRASS KNUCKLES, TOWEL, ROPE, ELBOW PADS...

JIM DAVIS

GARFIELD'S BATH DAY?

GARFIELD'S BATH DAY

SCRUB
SCRUB
SCRUB
SCRUB

2-18 JIM DAVIS

© 1979 United Feature Syndicate, Inc.

CLICK!

GARFIELD!
STOP!

IT'S BELOW
FREEZING
OUT THERE

BE HONEST, POOKY. DO YOU THINK I'M GETTING A LITTLE PUDGY AROUND THE MIDDLE?

2-21

NOT A LOT OF PERSONALITY, BUT HE CERTAINLY KNOWS WHEN TO KEEP HIS MOUTH SHUT

JIM DAVIS

© 1979 United Feature Syndicate, Inc.

2-22

A DANCING BEAR?

NEXT TIME, I GET TO LEAD

© 1979 United Feature Syndicate, Inc. JIM DAVIS

STAND ASIDE, CAT. I KNOW KARATE!

2-26

AND I KNOW FAST AND FURIOUS

JIM DAVIS

SOME DAYS I'M JUST NOT IN THE MOOD TO BE ADORED

JIM DAVIS

2-27

© 1979 United Feature Syndicate, Inc.

© 1979 United Feature Syndicate, Inc.

GARFIELD, THAT STEELY-EYED COWCAT, ROAMS INTO TOWN

© 1979 United Feature Syndicate, Inc.

3-9

HE MOUNTS HIS FAITHFUL STEED, ODIE

ALL I NEED NOW IS A SUNSET

JIM DAVIS

© 1979 United Feature Syndicate, Inc.

3-10

JUST WHEN YOU THINK YOU'VE SEEN YOUR CAT DO IT ALL...

JIM DAVIS

SWISH!

THE MOUTH IS QUICKER THAN THE HAND

© 1979 United Feature Syndicate, Inc.   3-12

JIM DAVIS

© 1979 United Feature Syndicate, Inc.

KNOCK! KNOCK! KNOCK!

NOBODY HOME

3-13

JIM DAVIS

I SUPPOSE I SHOULD LEARN TO LIKE ODIE

BUT I JUST CAN'T RESPECT ANYONE WHO TURNS AROUND THREE TIMES TO LIE DOWN

JIM DAVIS 3-14

© 1979 United Feature Syndicate, Inc. 3-15

HMMM

JUST AS I SUSPECTED. THERE'S A TINY SIGN IN THERE SAYING, "SPACE FOR RENT"

JIM DAVIS

HMMM, JON'S DRAWING BOARD. HMMM, SOME PAPER. HMMM, SOME INK

I THINK THIS WORLD WOULD BE A NICER PLACE IN WHICH TO LIVE:
IF COUNTRIES COULD SETTLE THEIR DIFFERENCES WITHOUT HURTING ANYBODY.
IF EVERYONE SMILED AT EVEN PEOPLE THEY DIDN'T KNOW

IF NOBODY HAD TO STEAL.
IF PEOPLE LAUGHED MORE.
IF EVERYONE FED THEIR CATS ALL THE LASAGNA THEY COULD EAT.
IF WE ALL TOOK MORE PRIDE IN OUR HOMES AND OUR NEIGHBORHOODS

© 1979 United Feature Syndicate, Inc.

3-18

IF WE RESPECTED OUR SENIOR CITIZENS MORE.
IF THERE WERE NO VIOLENCE IN MOVIES AND TELEVISION.
IF EVERYONE COULD READ AND WRITE.
IF FAMILIES TALKED MORE

IF FRIENDS HUGGED MORE.
IF EVERYONE STOPPED AT LEAST ONCE A WEEK TO STROKE A CAT.
AFTER ALL, WE'RE ALL IN THIS TOGETHER

HEY, GARFIELD

WHAT'S THIS?

OH, JUST SOME PAW PRINTS

JIM DAVIS

SIT UP AND BEG FOR THE KITTY MUNCHY, GARFIELD

3-23

TELL YOU WHAT. YOU GIVE ME THE MUNCHY AND I'LL LET YOU KEEP YOUR FACE

I KNEW WE COULD ARRIVE AT A MUTUALLY ACCEPTABLE COMPROMISE

JIM DAVIS © 1979 United Feature Syndicate, Inc.

DANCE FOR ME, GARFIELD

NOT A CHANCE

JIM DAVIS © 1979 United Feature Syndicate, Inc.

IF YOU WON'T, I'M SURE ODIE WOULD BE HAPPY TO

YOU HAVE TO KNOW WHAT MOTIVATES A CAT

THIS IS DEMEANING

TAPPITY TAPPITY

3-24

3-25 © 1979 United Feature Syndicate, Inc.

SIGH

HO HUM
GARFIELD

EVER HAD ONE OF THOSE DAYS WHEN YOU FEEL LIKE YOU'VE SLEPT AND EATEN IT ALL?

JIM DAVIS

AH, IT'S EARLY MORNING FOR THE CAPED AVENGER

RING!

THE CAPED AVENGER WHO SEARCHES OUT EVIL WHEREVER IT MAY LURK

THE LATE-MORNING EVIL, THAT IS

3-26

JIM DAVIS

© 1979 United Feature Syndicate, Inc.

THE CAPED AVENGER SEES FOOD!

© 1979 United Feature Syndicate, Inc.

3-27

IN ORDER TO FIGHT EVIL, THE CAPED AVENGER NEEDS FOOD FOR STRENGTH

LOTS AND **LOTS** OF STRENGTH!

JIM DAVIS

© 1979 United Feature Syndicate, Inc.

CLICK

I'M GOING TO STARE AT THIS TOASTER UNTIL THE TOAST POPS UP

A WATCHED POT NEVER BOILS, GARFIELD

HUH?

POP

© 1979 United Feature Syndicate, Inc.

SEE?

DRAT... DRAT, DRAT, DRAT, DRAT

JIM DAVIS

4-8

HMMMM

HERE, ODIE,

© 1979 United Feature Syndicate, Inc.

4-22

YIP!
YIP!
YIP!

JIM DAVIS

GARFIELD! GET OUT OF MY SOCK DRAWER!

4-23 © 1979 United Feature Syndicate, Inc.

CRASH!

IT'S AMAZING THE FUN YOU CAN HAVE WITH A HOOP

JIM DAVIS

GEE, I'D ALMOST FORGOTTEN HOW MUCH FUN IT IS TO HANG ON THE OLD SCREEN DOOR

4-24

SLAM!

© 1979 United Feature Syndicate, Inc.

AND I'D COMPLETELY FORGOTTEN ABOUT THE PAIN

JIM DAVIS

© 1979 United Feature Syndicate, Inc.   4-27

POP

THEY DON'T CALL ME "LIGHTNING LIPS" FOR NOTHING

JIM DAVIS

I JUST WANT YOU PEOPLE TO KNOW HOW MUCH WE CATS APPRECIATE YOU. WITHOUT YOU, WHO WOULD FEED US? WHO WOULD LOVE US?

4-28

AND MOST IMPORTANT OF ALL...

WHO WOULD CHANGE OUR KITTY LITTER?

JIM DAVIS   © 1979 United Feature Syndicate, Inc.

GROWL

THE CAT CRAVES FRESH MEAT

4-29

WHAT-HO, THE CAT SENSES UNSUSPECTING QUARRY O'ER YON KNOLL

© 1979 United Feature Syndicate, Inc.

JIM DAVIS

COILING LIKE A SPRING, HE PREPARES TO LUNGE

STEELY SINEWS PROPEL HIM TOWARD HIS HELPLESS PREY

ONCE AGAIN A CAT'S PRIMAL INSTINCTS PROVIDE SUSTENANCE

BURP!

5-2

THAT WAS RUDE AND CRUDE, GARFIELD. CATS ARE MORE SOPHISTICATED THAN TO SUBMIT TO BELCHING AT THE DINNER TABLE

BRAACK!

JIM DAVIS © 1979 United Feature Syndicate, Inc.

TELL ME WHAT YOU THINK OF MY NEW POEM, GARFIELD

5-3

"MY BUDDY"
I HAVE A BUDDY.
MY BUDDY'S A TOAD.
HE'S KIND OF MUDDY,
HE'S FLAT ON THE ROAD.
BUT, HE IS MY BUDDY,
MY BUDDY TO STAY.
'TIL HE'S PEELED UP
AND SAILED AWAY

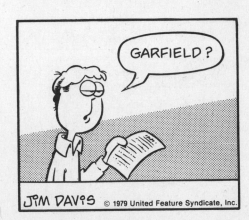

GARFIELD?

JIM DAVIS © 1979 United Feature Syndicate, Inc.

UH-OH, HERE COMES JON!

5-4

ARE YOU HUNGRY, ODIE?

© 1979 United Feature Syndicate, Inc.

HERE, HAVE SOME CELERY AND TOMATOES AND RADISHES

GARFIELD!

5-5

JIM DAVIS

EAT UP, OL' BUDDY

HMMMM

YOU WON'T GET RID OF ME THAT EASILY!

5-13

JIM DAVIS

NOW WHAT DID I DO?

© 1979 United Feature Syndicate, Inc.

© 1979 United Feature Syndicate, Inc. 5-18

AT LAST! MY FEET CAN TOUCH THE FLOOR ONCE MORE

JIM DAVIS 5-19

NEVER AGAIN WILL I ALLOW MYSELF TO GET THAT FAT

© 1979 United Feature Syndicate, Inc.

AND IF YOU BELIEVE THAT, I HAVE A BRIDGE TO SELL YOU

© 1979 United Feature Syndicate, Inc.

GARFIELD, YOU'VE BEEN IN BED ALL WEEK. WHY, YOU COULD STARVE TO DEATH

© 1979 United Feature Syndicate, Inc.

OH

I SHOULD HAVE GUESSED AS MUCH

6-1

JIM DAVIS

GET OUT OF BED THIS MINUTE, GARFIELD

JIM DAVIS

6-2

GOOD BOY!

DARN LEG CRAMPS

© 1979 United Feature Syndicate, Inc.

HEY, LYMAN. WHAT DO YOU THINK OF MY NEW TENNIS RACKET?

WHAT'S IT STRUNG WITH?

CATGUT

6-6

© 1979 United Feature Syndicate, Inc.

AUNT REBA!

JIM DAVIS

THAT'S THE TROUBLE WITH WARM WEATHER

JIM DAVIS

YOU CAN'T KEEP ICE CUBES IN YOUR DRINK

© 1979 United Feature Syndicate, Inc.

6-7

SCREW
SCREW
SCREW

LOOK, GARFIELD!
I MADE A
KITTY DOOR
FOR YOU

© 1979 United Feature Syndicate, Inc.

SWING

SMACK!

SMASH!

A CLEAR-CUT CASE
OF SELF-DEFENSE IF
I EVER SAW ONE

JIM DAVIS

6-17

FOOD!

WHAT'S THIS?

IT APPEARS TO BE OF THE CRESCENT ROLL FAMILY

A TRUE GOURMET NEVER SHIES AWAY FROM A NEW TASTE TREAT

© 1979 United Feature Syndicate, Inc.

(SMACK) A BIT DRY, BUT PALATABLE

GARFIELD, HAVE YOU SEEN MY SWEAT SOCKS?

JIM DAVIS

7-8

CATCH THE ROPE, GARFIELD!

© 1979 United Feature Syndicate, Inc.

NOW TIE IT AROUND YOUR WAIST AND I'LL PULL YOU DOWN. HA-HA-HA!

I'LL GET JON FOR THAT

7-11

JIM DAVIS

I'VE COME TO RESCUE YOU, GARFIELD

JIM DAVIS

UH-OH

WELL, THIS IS JUST DUCKY

7-12 © 1979 United Feature Syndicate, Inc.

THERE'S ONLY ONE WAY OUT OF THIS TREE, GARFIELD

7-13 JiM DAViS

WE'LL HAVE TO JUMP

GEE, I'D LOVE TO BUT I SIMPLY HAVEN'T A THING TO WEAR TO OUR FUNERAL

© 1979 United Feature Syndicate, Inc.

EITHER WE JUMP, OR WE'LL STARVE UP HERE, GARFIELD

I'M WITH YOU

JiM DAViS

GERONIMO!!

© 1979 United Feature Syndicate, Inc.

7-14

ZOOM!

© 1979 United Feature Syndicate, Inc.   7-16

WHY, OH WHY, OH WHY, OH WHY, DO CATS DO THESE THINGS?

JIM DAVIS

I'M GETTING OUT OF THIS TREE IF IT KILLS ME

7-17

POOMP!

GEE, THAT DIDN'T HURT AT ALL

JIM DAVIS

GO GET 'IM, GARFIELD!

OOPS!

SQUEAK!

EVERYONE STAND BACK! GIVE HIM SOME AIR!

ARTIFICIAL RESPIRATION MIGHT HELP

7-22   © 1979 United Feature Syndicate, Inc.

OKAY GO, BOY

PHEW! FOR A MINUTE THERE I THOUGHT I WAS OUT OF A JOB

JIM DAVIS

TELL ME, DOCTOR, WHAT DO YOU SUGGEST FOR AN ANIMAL WHO'S MADLY IN LOVE?

JIM DAVIS

I USUALLY PRESCRIBE NEUTERING

7-27

© 1979 United Feature Syndicate, Inc.

WE'LL MAKE AN APPOINTMENT FOR GARFIELD'S NEXT CHECK-UP IN ABOUT SIX MONTHS

7-28   JIM DAVIS

WHAT IF THERE'S AN EMERGENCY?

THEN YOU CAN CALL ME DAY OR NIGHT

© 1979 United Feature Syndicate, Inc.

COME ON, GARFIELD. LET'S GO HOME AND PLAY IN TRAFFIC

THAT'S NOT FUNNY

7-30

ZOOM!

HOW DO THEY KNOW WHEN IT'S BATH DAY?

JIM DAVIS © 1979 United Feature Syndicate, Inc.

BATH TIME!

© 1979 United Feature Syndicate, Inc.

7-31

CHUCKLE CHUCKLE

OKAY, WHO PUT OATMEAL IN THE SOAPBOX?

WELL, SPRINKLE ME WITH BROWN SUGAR AND CALL ME FOR BREAKFAST

JIM DAVIS

BOING BOING BOING

NG BOING BOING

8-3

HELP!

BOING BOING

© 1979 United Feature Syndicate, Inc. JIM DAVIS

FOR STAYING OUT OF MY FOOD TODAY, GARFIELD, I'M GOING TO REWARD YOU WITH A KITTY MUNCHIE

© 1979 United Feature Syndicate, Inc.

8-4

THEY'RE GONE

I ALREADY REWARDED MYSELF

JIM DAVIS

8-5

WHAT SAY I SWITCH OVER TO THE MOVIE, GANG?

NAH GRRR FFFT

JIM DAVIS

GARFIELD'S HISTORY OF CATS: THE VERY FIRST CAT CRAWLED OUT OF THE SEA ABOUT TEN MILLION YEARS AGO

8-6

FORTUNATELY FOR HIM...

IT WAS ONLY ABOUT ANOTHER 15 MINUTES BEFORE THE FIRST MOUSE CRAWLED OUT

JIM DAVIS © 1979 United Feature Syndicate, Inc.

GARFIELD'S HISTORY OF CATS: THE FIRST CAT WAS DOMESTICATED ABOUT A MILLION YEARS AGO. THE CAT (NAMED "ORG") WAS OWNED BY A CAVE MAN NAMED "CHUCK"

8-7

WHILE RUMOR HAS IT THAT ORG ATE HIS OWNER...

© 1979 United Feature Syndicate, Inc.

HISTORIANS MAINTAIN THE FAMILY DOG ATE CHUCK

JIM DAVIS

GARFIELD'S HISTORY OF CATS: DURING THE DARK AGES THE LEGENDARY RATTER "FLUFFY-THE-FIERCE" DESTROYED EVERY RAT BUT ONE...

SQUEAK!

OL' FLUFFY GOT HIS CLOCK CLEANED BY THE EVEN MORE LEGENDARY "MATT-THE-RAT"

DRIBBLE
DRIBBLE
DRIBBLE

INCIDENTALLY, IT WAS MATT-THE-RAT WHO COINED THE TERM "HERE, KITTY, KITTY, KITTY"

© 1979 United Feature Syndicate, Inc.   8-8

GARFIELD'S HISTORY OF CATS: MARCO POLO HAD A CAT NAMED ROLO

ROLO POLO

8-9   © 1979 United Feature Syndicate, Inc.

ROLO WOULD HAVE GONE WITH MARCO ON HIS TRIP TO THE ORIENT...

BUT MOTELS WOULDN'T ACCEPT PETS THEN

WAH!

JIM DAVIS

GARFIELD'S HISTORY OF CATS:
A CAT DISCOVERED AMERICA!

IT WAS CHRISTOPHER COLUMBUS' CAT "BUCKEYE" WHO FIRST SPOTTED THE BEACH

PRIMARILY BECAUSE THE SANTA MARIA DIDN'T HAVE A SANDBOX

8-10 JIM DAVIS

© 1979 United Feature Syndicate, Inc.

GARFIELD'S HISTORY OF CATS:
CATS' PENCHANT FOR SHARPENING THEIR CLAWS HAS SERVED MANY HISTORIC PURPOSES: IN VICTORIAN TIMES CATS WERE USED TO ANTIQUE FURNITURE

RRRRRRR

8-11

DURING THE SPANISH-AMERICAN WAR, CATS WERE USED AS INTERROGATORS

I'LL TALK! I'LL TALK!

© 1979 United Feature Syndicate, Inc.

AND TODAY, THE POST OFFICE USES CATS TO SORT MAIL MARKED "FRAGILE"

JIM DAVIS

ZOOM!

YOU WIN. YOU WERE UGLIER TO BEGIN WITH

JIM DAVIS

I'M NEVER TAKING YOU GOLFING AGAIN, GARFIELD

BIG DEAL

I'VE NEVER BEEN SO EMBARRASSED

I CAN'T BELIEVE WHAT YOU DID AT THE SEVENTEENTH GREEN

SAND TRAP, SANDBOX, WHAT'S THE DIFFERENCE?

JIM DAVIS

© 1979 United Feature Syndicate, Inc.   8-24

© 1979 United Feature Syndicate, Inc.   8-25

A Talk with Jim Davis:
Most Asked Questions

How far in advance do you do the strip?

"Eight to ten weeks—no less, no more. I operate on what Al Capp termed 'the ragged edge of disaster.'"

When did GARFIELD first appear in newspapers?

"June 19, 1978."

Do you own a cat? A GARFIELD?

"No. My wife, Carolyn, is allergic to cats. However, I did grow up on a farm with about 25 cats."

Where do you get your ideas for the strip?

"I glean a lot of good ideas from fan mail. Cat owners are very proud of their cats and supply a generous amount of cat stories."

What GARFIELD products are on the market and in production?

"Books, calendars, T-shirts, coffee mugs, posters, tote bags, greeting cards, puzzles…in another few months GARFIELD will be on everything but pantyhose and TVs."

Why a cat?

"Aside from the obvious reasons, that I know and love cats, I noticed there were a lot of comic-strip dogs who were commanding their share of the comic pages but precious few cats. It seemed like a good idea."

Where did you get the name GARFIELD?

"My grandfather's name was James A. Garfield Davis. The name GARFIELD to me sounds like a fat cat…or a St. Bernard…or a neat line of thermal underwear."

What did you do for a living before GARFIELD?

"I was assistant on the comic strip TUMBLEWEEDS and a free-lance commercial artist."

What's your sign?

"Leo, of course, the sign of the cat."

Have you ever been convicted of a felony?

"Next question, please."

Are you subject to fainting spells, seizures, and palpitations?

"Only when I work."

Have you ever spent time in a mental institution?

"Yes, I visit my comics editor there."

Do you advocate the overthrow of our government by violent means?

"No, but I have given consideration to vandalizing my local license branch."

Are you hard of hearing?

"Huh?"

Do you wish to donate an organ?

"Heck no, but I have a piano I can let go cheap."

Garfield bigger than life

BY: JiM DAViS

how to draw Garfield

1.

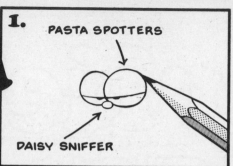

PASTA SPOTTERS

DAISY SNIFFER

2.

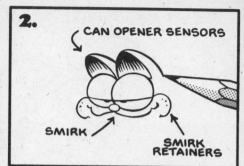

CAN OPENER SENSORS

SMIRK

SMIRK RETAINERS

3.

STROKING SURFACE

LASAGNA STORAGE UNITS

TWITCHER

4.

HAIR BALL CATCHER

DIRT DRAGGER

CHAIR SHREDDERS

5.

NOT JUST ANOTHER PRETTY FACE

STRIPES

NOW ADD THE PERSONALITY

JIM DAVIS

OH, GREAT

GARFIELD ATE MY TOOTHPASTE AGAIN

JIM DAVIS

8-29

I JUST **LOVE** TO COURT DANGER

8-30

SPLOOSH!

YIPEEE, HA-HA, WHEEE

JIM DAVIS

THIS IS MY PET ANT, LYLE. HE'S CUTE, QUIET, AND INDUSTRIOUS

SPLAT!

THE "LATE" LYLE WAS ALSO EYEBALLING MY LASAGNA

WHAT?! WHERE?!

HE DID IT AGAIN

JIM DAVIS

SCUFFLE
SCUFFLE
STRUGGLE
GRAB!
STUFF
STUFF

GUESS WHAT, GARFIELD? WHILE MOM AND DAD'RE ON A WEEK'S VACATION, WE'RE GOING TO BABY-SIT FOR THEIR KITTEN

9-3

MEET NERMAL

WAKE ME IN A WEEK

© 1979 United Feature Syndicate, Inc.

JIM DAVIS

I GOTTA SPEND A WEEK WET-NURSING NERMAL, HERE... HE'S CUTE

9-4   © 1979 United Feature Syndicate, Inc.

AND I HATE "CUTE"

JIM DAVIS

DON'T KNOCK IT, JACK. I MAKE A KILLING POSING FOR GREETING CARDS

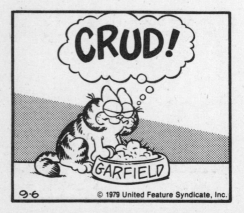

TAKE THOSE ROLLER SKATES OFF, GARFIELD. YOU LOOK RIDICULOUS

9-7

JIM DAVIS

NERMAL'S LEAVING NOW. WAVE BYE-BYE, GARFIELD

9-8

I KIND OF LIKED THE LITTLE FELLER

THE WAY I LIKE INTESTINAL FLU

JIM DAVIS

SPLOOSH!

OH-NO! A VICIOUS UNDERTOW IS DRAGGING ME OUT TO SEA!

I'M TOO YOUNG TO GO!

9-9

I CAN SEE THE HEADLINES NOW... "WORLD FAMOUS CAT LOST AT SEA. MILLIONS OF BEAUTIFUL GIRL CATS GRIEF-STRICKEN!"

I CAN'T MAKE IT! I'M GOING DOWN FOR THE THIRD TIME!

© 1979 United Feature Syndicate, Inc.

I'D SAVE YOU, GARFIELD. BUT I'M NOT ABOUT TO GIVE A CAT MOUTH-TO-MOUTH RESUSCITATION

JIM DAVIS

YAWN

9-10
© 1979 United Feature Syndicate, Inc.

OH, THIS LOOKS LIKE A NICE PLACE TO SLEEP

IF YOU DON'T MIND, GARFIELD..

JIM DAVIS

SACK! PILLAGE! MAIM! DESTROY!

9-11

BONK!

WHIMPER, LIMP, CRY, HURT, MOAN

JIM DAVIS
© 1979 United Feature Syndicate, Inc.

SMACK
MUNCH
SLURP

CLICK!

9-16

ZZZ

I DIDN'T KNOW CATS COULD EAT IN THEIR SLEEP

JIM DAVIS

BUT I DO KNOW THEY CAN'T SHARPEN THEIR CLAWS IN THEIR SLEEP

I SHOULDN'T HAVE PUSHED IT

© 1979 United Feature Syndicate, Inc.

ATTENTION AMERICA! I AM HEREBY DECLARING THIS WEEK **NATIONAL FAT WEEK**

© 1979 United Feature Syndicate, Inc.

THIS IS THE WEEK FOR ALL YOU FAT PEOPLE TO COME OUT OF THE CLOSET

9-17

THOSE OF YOU WHO COULD GET INTO ONE, THAT IS

JIM DAVIS

THIS IS NATIONAL FAT WEEK. I WANT TO HEAR ALL YOU FAT PEOPLE SAY, "I'M FAT, AND I'M PROUD OF IT!"

© 1979 United Feature Syndicate, Inc.   JIM DAVIS

LOUDER! "I'M FAT, AND I'M PROUD OF IT!"

9-18

YOU...THE PUDGY ONE IN SEATTLE, I DIDN'T HEAR YOU

HERE'S A NATIONAL FAT WEEK HANDY FAT TIP

© 1979 United Feature Syndicate, Inc.

"DON'T EXERCISE." YOU'LL BE HAPPIER

HAVE YOU EVER SEEN A JOGGER LAUGH?

9-19   JIM DAVIS

HERE'S A NATIONAL FAT WEEK SKINNY JOKE

9-20   JIM DAVIS

HOW MANY SKINNY PEOPLE DOES IT TAKE TO FILL A SHOWER?

I DON'T KNOW. THEY KEEP SLIPPING DOWN THE DRAIN

© 1979 United Feature Syndicate, Inc.

HERE'S THE NATIONAL FAT WEEK "WEIGHT-HEIGHT CHART"

ACCORDING TO THIS, IF YOU WEIGH 200 POUNDS, YOU SHOULD BE 6'4"

9-21

THAT MEANS IF YOU'RE UNDER 6'4" YOU'RE NOT OVERWEIGHT, YOU'RE UNDERTALL

JIM DAVIS

WELL, FAT BROTHERS AND SISTERS, THIS IS THE LAST DAY OF NATIONAL FAT WEEK

9-22

JUST REMEMBER, "ROUND IS BEAUTIFUL"

NOW GET OUT THERE AND EAT A CHICKEN FRANCHISE

JIM DAVIS

© 1979 United Feature Syndicate, Inc.

BE CAREFUL THERE, GARFIELD

© 1979 United Feature Syndicate, Inc.

HANGING ON THE DRAPES CAN BE VERY PAINFUL

'CAUSE I'M GONNA BREAK YOUR LEGS IF YOU DON'T GET OFF THEM THIS INSTANT!

9-24

GASP! CHOKE! WHEEZE!

9-25

OH NO YOU DON'T, GARFIELD

SO MUCH FOR THE OLD "PLAY-SICK-AND-GRAB-THE-CHICKEN-WHEN-YOUR-OWNER-CALLS-THE-VET" ROUTINE

JIM DAVIS © 1979 United Feature Syndicate, Inc.

GARFIELD! BREAKFAST!

9-26

BONK!

I DID IT AGAIN. I GOT UP BEFORE I WOKE UP

© 1979 United Feature Syndicate, Inc. JIM DAVIS

WAG WAG WAG

© 1979 United Feature Syndicate, Inc.

STOMP!

WAG WAG WAG

9-27 JIM DAVIS

9-30

OH, DARN

JON'S FLOWER GARDEN GOT A LITTLE OVER-FROLICKED

JIM DAVIS   © 1979 United Feature Syndicate, Inc.

WE'RE GOING TO SEE YOUR VETERINARIAN TODAY, GARFIELD

10-1

SHE'S ONE CUTE CHICKY-BOO. I'D MARRY HER IN A SECOND

© 1979 United Feature Syndicate, Inc.

IT'S COMFORTING TO KNOW THE HIGH VALUES PLACED ON THE SACRED INSTITUTION OF MARRIAGE ARE STILL WITH US TODAY

IN A HALF-SECOND!

JIM DAVIS

© 1979 United Feature Syndicate, Inc.

THAT LIZ IS SURE A GREAT LOOKING HUNK OF VETERINARIAN

SHE HAS THE ONE QUALITY I DESIRE MOST IN A WOMAN

SHE'S BREATHING

10-2

JIM DAVIS

BE RIGHT WITH YOU, MR. ARBUCKLE

© 1979 United Feature Syndicate, Inc.

I'LL BE HERE WITH BELLS ON, DOCTOR

THAT MAKES FOR AN INTERESTING MENTAL PICTURE

WHY DOES SHE ALWAYS PUT ME DOWN?

YOU'RE SO PUTDOWNABLE

10·3

JIM DAVIS

HOW ABOUT GOING OUT WITH ME, DOCTOR?

I WOULDN'T GO OUT WITH YOU IF YOU WERE THE LAST MAN ON EARTH

10·4

THEN HOW ABOUT SOMETIME AFTER THAT?

THAT'S A GOOD ONE

JIM DAVIS   © 1979 United Feature Syndicate, Inc.

MY AUNT EVELYN IS THE NEATEST CAT I KNOW

© 1979 United Feature Syndicate, Inc.   10-10

SHE PLUCKED ALL THE HAIR OFF HER BODY SO SHE WOULDN'T SHED ON THE FURNITURE

NOW SHE'S LIVING WITH A FAMILY IN L.A. THAT THINKS SHE'S A CHIHUAHUA

JIM DAVIS

YIP! YIP! YIP!

© 1979 United Feature Syndicate, Inc.

YIP! YIP! YIP!

FOR THE LAST TIME, ODIE, **YOU** CHASE THE **TAIL**

10-11   JIM DAVIS

GARFIELD, MUST YOU DO EVERYTHING I DO?

10-12

THAT WASN'T VERY NICE

AFTER ALL, CATS ARE JUST LITTLE PEOPLE WITH FUR AND FANGS

JIM DAVIS © 1979 United Feature Syndicate, Inc.

© 1979 United Feature Syndicate, Inc. 10-13

FWIP FWIP FWIP FWIP FWIP FWIP SHOOP!

A VENETIAN TONGUE

JIM DAVIS

SMACK!

10·22

I HATE PATIO DOORS

JIM DAVIS

10-23 © 1979 United Feature Syndicate, Inc.

HEY, GARFIELD, WHERE'S ODIE?

HE'S EASY ENOUGH TO FIND

JIM DAVIS

JUST FOLLOW THE SLOBBER

© 1979 United Feature Syndicate, Inc.

WHEN I THINK OF SAND, I THINK OF SUN, SURF AND GETTING A GOOD TAN

WHAT DO YOU THINK OF WHEN YOU THINK OF SAND, GARFIELD?

11-9 © 1979 United Feature Syndicate, Inc.

ON SECOND THOUGHT, SCRATCH THAT QUESTION

JIM DAVIS

11-10 © 1979 United Feature Syndicate, Inc.

FRED'S FRESH FISH

FRED'S FRESH FISH

JIM DAVIS

rain (rān) *n.* **1.** water falling to earth in drops

2. a mild depressant

JIM DAVIS © 1979 United Feature Syndicate, Inc.

© 1979 United Feature Syndicate, Inc.

ZZZZ

SCREECH!

CHASING CARS AGAIN, GARFIELD?

JIM DAVIS   11-13

AH-AH-AH

AHCHOO!

© 1979 United Feature Syndicate, Inc.

SNIFF

11-19

JIM DAVIS

SCRATCH THE SOFA ALL YOU LIKE, GARFIELD

REVERSE PSYCHOLOGY

JIM DAVIS

© 1979 United Feature Syndicate, Inc.

REVERSE REVERSE PSYCHOLOGY

11-20

I OFTEN WONDER WHAT GOES ON IN THAT COMPLEX MIND OF YOURS, GARFIELD

BZZZZZZZZZZZZZ

WOULDN'T IT BE WONDERFUL IF HUMANS AND ANIMALS COULD COMMUNICATE?

SMACK!

JIM DAVIS
© 1979 United Feature Syndicate, Inc.

WHAT WOULD YOU SAY TO ME IF YOU COULD TALK RIGHT NOW?

I JUST KILLED A FLY SOMEWHERE ON YOUR RAISIN TOAST

11-23

THAT'S A NASTY COLD YOU HAVE THERE, GARFIELD

SNIFF

© 1979 United Feature Syndicate, Inc.

WE'LL TAKE YOU TO THE VET AND GET YOU FIXED RIGHT UP

JIM DAVIS

NEVER SAY "FIXED" TO AN ANIMAL PERSON

11-24

GET OFF THE CEILING, GARFIELD

GET OUT OF THE GLOVE COMPARTMENT, GARFIELD

© 1979 United Feature Syndicate, Inc.

GET BACK IN THE GLOVE COMPARTMENT, GARFIELD

11-26

© 1979 United Feature Syndicate, Inc.

GET YOUR FACE OFF THE WINDSHIELD, GARFIELD

11-27

HAVE YOU EVER NOTICED HOW MUCH SOME PEOPLE LOOK LIKE THEIR PETS, GARFIELD?

HEE HEE

HEE

HA·HA HA

HA

12-2

JIM DAVIS

GUESS WHO'S COME TO VISIT US THIS WEEK, GARFIELD?

NERMAL! THE WORLD'S CUTEST KITTEN

YOU'RE TESTING ME, AREN'T YOU?!

© 1979 United Feature Syndicate, Inc. JIM DAVIS

HOW CUTE!

JIM DAVIS

© 1979 United Feature Syndicate, Inc.

12-3

12-4

GET OFF THE PIANO, ODIE. YOU'RE MAKING TOO MUCH RACKET

AND YOU...

12-12

GARFIELD! THAT'S BEAUTIFUL!

WE'LL GO ON THE ROAD. WE'LL MAKE A MILLION! WE'RE RICH!

© 1979 United Feature Syndicate, Inc.

12-13

STOP PLAYING WITH THE FLASHLIGHT, GARFIELD

CLICK!

12-14

JIM DAVIS

© 1979 United Feature Syndicate, Inc.

JIM DAVIS

YOUR PICTURE 4 FOR 50¢

12-15

© 1979 United Feature Syndicate, Inc.

© 1979 United Feature Syndicate, Inc. JIM DAVIS

UH-OH! HERE COMES JON!

THE PERFECT CRIME

OH, GARFIELD

HAVE YOU, PERCHANCE, SEEN MY CHICKEN?

12-23

12-24 © 1979 United Feature Syndicate, Inc.

12-25

JIM DAVIS © 1979 United Feature Syndicate, Inc.

© 1979 United Feature Syndicate, Inc.

12-28

SPIDERS ARE CURIOUS INSECTS TO SEE. THEIR WEBS ARE REALLY NEAT.

BUT HOW DO THEY WEAVE THEM ELABORATELY, WHEN ALL THEY HAVE IS FEET?

JIM DAVIS

GARFIELD AND I CAN ACTUALLY COMMUNICATE. WATCH THIS...

WOULD YOU LIKE TO TAKE A BATH, GARFIELD?

12-29

GARFIELD SAID "NO"

© 1979 United Feature Syndicate, Inc.

JIM DAVIS

CRASH!

GARFIELD! YOU BROKE MY FERN!!

© 1979 United Feature Syndicate, Inc.

I RAISED THAT FERN FROM A FROND!

12-30

WHAT DID THAT FERN EVER DO TO YOU?!!

WHY, I HAVE A NOTION TO...UH...TO

I...UH

YOU'RE SO CUTE

LIKE PUTTY IN MY PAWS

JIM DAVIS

BACK OFF, GARFIELD. THAT TURKEY LEG IS FOR MY LUNCH

AHCHOO!

WIPE
WIPE
WIPE
WIPE

SCRATCH
SCRATCH
SCRATCH
SCRATCH
SCRATCH
SCRATCH

© 1980 United Feature Syndicate, Inc

1-6

WOULD YOU LIKE A TURKEY LEG, GARFIELD?

ONLY IF YOU DON'T WANT IT

JIM DAVIS

YIP!

PUNT!

1-9

JIM DAVIS

THROW ME A ROLL, JON

GULP!

1-10

JIM DAVIS

PASS ME A ROLL, JON

1-13

© 1980 United Feature Syndicate, Inc

JiM DAVIS

I THOUGHT SO

SNIFF

© 1980 United Feature Syndicate, Inc.   1-18

ARRRGH!!!

COLDS CAN BE FRUSTRATING CAN'T THEY, OL' BUDDY?

JIM DAVIS

YOUR COUGH SOUNDS BETTER, GARFIELD

HACK HACK

© 1980 United Feature Syndicate, Inc.

IT SHOULD

1-19

I'VE BEEN PRACTICING ALL NIGHT

JIM DAVIS

© 1980 United Feature Syndicate, Inc.

1-20

JIM DAVIS

MORNING, LIZ. JON HERE. I'M BRINGING GARFIELD IN FOR A CHECKUP TODAY

© 1980 United Feature Syndicate, Inc.

I KNOW YOU'VE BEEN WANTING TO GET TO KNOW ME BETTER, SO WHY DON'T YOU MAKE IT A LATE APPOINTMENT AND WE'LL GO TO DINNER AFTERWARD

1-28

JON... JON ARBUCKLE

JIM DAVIS

HI, DOCTOR! REMEMBER ME? JON? YOUR KNIGHT IN SHINING ARMOR?

© 1980 United Feature Syndicate, Inc.   1-29

OH YES, I REMEMBER

NAMES ESCAPE ME, BUT I NEVER FORGET A TWIT

JIM DAVIS

HELP YOURSELF, GARFIELD

2-6

WOULD YOU LIKE A LITTLE COFFEE IN THAT SUGAR?

JIM DAVIS © 1980 United Feature Syndicate, Inc.

THIS SHOULD BLOW JON'S MIND. ME, GARFIELD, BEING NICE TO ODIE

PAT PAT

2-7

HEH HEH, HOW NICE

PAT PAT

THAT WAS A JOKE, YOU TWIT

JIM DAVIS © 1980 United Feature Syndicate, Inc.

PUSH!

THIS TABLE WASN'T BIG ENOUGH FOR THE BOTH OF US

JIM DAVIS

POOMP!

OOPS. I CRUNCHED JON'S ANTENNA

A LITTLE MORE TO THE RIGHT, GARFIELD

WATCH THIS. I'M GOING TO SWING DOWN ON THIS VINE AND SWOOP UP JON'S CHICKEN

YANK YANK

SWOOP!

JIM DAVIS

WHERE DID THE VINE COME FROM?

© 1980 United Feature Syndicate, Inc.

2-10

2-17   JIM DAVIS

THE CAPED AVENGER SEES AN EVIL DOG

THE CAPED AVENGER SPRINGS INTO ACTION

2-20

THE CAPED AVENGER HURTS HIMSELF

© 1980 United Feature Syndicate, Inc.

2-21

© 1980 United Feature Syndicate, Inc.

SWIPE!

THANKS, GARFIELD. I HATE TO LICK STAMPS

BLUH, BLUH

JIM DAVIS

IT'S NOT THE HAVING,
IT'S THE GETTING

2 24

JIM DAVIS

B-R-R-R-R

2-29 © 1980 United Feature Syndicate, Inc.

AWWW, POOR THING. FIRST YOU'RE ON A DIET, NOW YOU'RE FREEZING

WHERE'S YOUR BLANKET?

I ATE IT

JIM DAVIS

YOU'RE LOOKING TRIMMER, GARFIELD. I'LL TAKE YOU OFF YOUR DIET NOW

31 JIM DAVIS

© 1980 United Feature Syndicate, Inc.

WHEW!

POOMP!

OH NO, YOU DON'T, GARFIELD. THIS CHICKEN LEG IS MINE

3·2

LET'S HEAR IT FOR CLAWS

© 1980 United Feature Syndicate, Inc

JIM DAVIS

THIS LOOKS LIKE IT'S GOING TO BE A GOOD WEEK

JIM DAVIS
© 1980 United Feature Syndicate, Inc.

NUTS... NUTS, NUTS, NUTS

3-10

MEYOW

© 1980 United Feature Syndicate, Inc.   3-11

LISTEN TO THAT

PURRR

THE KID'S A WALKING CLICHE

FFFT

JIM DAVIS

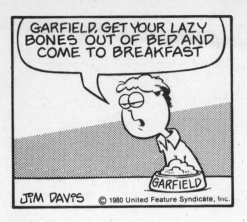

I KNOW YOU CATS ARE INQUISITIVE BY NATURE, GARFIELD

© 1980 United Feature Syndicate, Inc.

AND I KNOW THIS IS YOUR HOME AS WELL AS MINE...

BUT STAY OUT OF MY UNDERWEAR DRAWER!!

3-19   JIM DAVIS

COMPUTERS... EVERYTHING IS CONTROLLED BY COMPUTERS THESE DAYS

© 1980 United Feature Syndicate, Inc.

THAT CHICKEN YOU ATE WAS EVEN RAISED BY A COMPUTER

3-20

burp

JIM DAVIS

GUESS WHAT, GARFIELD? I'M ENTERING YOU IN A CAT SHOW

3-24   © 1980 United Feature Syndicate, Inc.

THAT SHOULD BE FUN...

I'LL BE DYNAMITE IN THE SWIMSUIT COMPETITION

JIM DAViS

YOU'LL HAVE TO TAKE A BATH BEFORE THE CAT SHOW, GARFIELD

I'LL TAKE MY CHANCES

3-25

CLEAN CATS ARE WINNING CATS

THE THINGS I DO FOR STARDOM

© 1980 United Feature Syndicate, Inc.   JIM DAViS

NOW LET'S FLUFF YOU UP

3-26

RRRRRR

© 1980 United Feature Syndicate, Inc.   JIM DAVIS

WE NEED A GIMMICK FOR THE CAT SHOW, GARFIELD, SOMETHING TO MAKE THE JUDGE NOTICE YOU

3-27

THIS SHOULD DO IT

IT'S A SAD STATE OF AFFAIRS WHEN A PET OWNER STOOPS TO HUMILIATING A CAT

JIM DAVIS   © 1980 United Feature Syndicate, Inc.

3-28

© 1980 United Feature Syndicate, Inc.

3-29

© 1980 United Feature Syndicate, Inc.

Garfield Up Close and Personal

Q: What is your favorite sport?
A: *Each morning, before breakfast, I like to take a good, brisk nap.*

Q: Where did you get your nasty temper, and why are you so cynical?
A: *Step a little closer and ask that.*

JIM DAVIS

Q: Describe your relationship with Jon, Odie, Pooky, and Nermal.
A: *Someone to abuse, someone to pound on, someone to confide in, and no comment.*

Q: Why did you call your most recent book "GARFIELD Bigger Than Life"?
A: *I didn't name the book, actually. I have the distinct feeling it is some kind of slur on my size. The book was named by my late editor.*

Q: How much money did you get for this book?
A: *Heavens to Betsy, I'm just a cat. That sort of thing doesn't concern me. Ask my agent.*

Q: Now that you are a success, do you give yourself your own baths?
A: *No, I've hired a cat to take baths for me.*

Q: Are you a prima donna?
A: *Not really.*

Q: Is there anyone with whom you would like to share the credit for your success?
A: *Not really.*